Gaining Control of Your Emotions

Quishauna Hairston

ISBN: 9798699689552

Gain: the act of acquiring something.

Control: to have power over.

Emotion: a state of feeling; a conscious mental reaction.

Sometimes it is hard for some of us to just allow ourselves to feel anything. To gain control over your emotions, you must first learn to be comfortable with feeling them and embracing them for what they are. Accept the things that you cannot change and become the change that you need.

Gaining control of your emotions is broken down into three key factors. Identifying the Problem, Developing

Coping Skills, and Change of Environment. Once you have invested in all three, there are no limits to the positive changes you can make in your life.

Content

Reasons

A cause, explanation, or justification for an action or event

to Smile

A pleased, kind, or amused facial expression

Life would be easy if we came with an instruction manual on how to identify the source of all our problems. Sadly, that is not the case. We are forced to dig deep inside ourselves to find out what is the root of our angry, sadness, resentment, frustration, etc.

I'm sure we could all write a book on everything that we feel is wrong in our lives. But first I want you to take a moment to identify everything right.

In the lines provided, make a list of everything that makes you happy, smile, joyful, motivated, excited, etc.

Triggers

A stimulus such as a smell, sound, or sight that bring back feelings of trauma

&

Emotions

a state of feeling; a conscious mental reaction.

The purpose of focusing on everything right is to help you train and reprogram your mind. You can gain control of what you choose to focus on.

Whenever you find yourself in a dark or empty space, you have something to reflect on to refocus your energy. Positive thoughts create positive results

Before we jump into identify the source, let's start by identifying what triggers you and how each trigger makes you feel. In the chart, write your triggers and describes how it makes you feel in one word.

Triggers	Emotions

Memories

Something remembered from the past

Understanding how each trigger makes you feel is a major step to finding the core factor. After identifying your triggers and emotions, you should be able to connect them to the event(s) that created the negative emotion in you.

In the next sections, I would like for you to journal about your memories that are tied to these emotions. This is the source.

Coping Skills

Any characteristic or behavioral pattern that enhances a person's adaption

Now that the root of the source(s) has been identified. The next step is learning to cope with it. To overcome things that have kept you bound you must learn to control it by using coping mechanisms. By practicing coping skills, your reaction whenever you are faced with something that can trigger a shift in your emotions, will no longer have a strong effect on you. It will eventually become natural to you. Therefore, you will have an extreme level of control over your emotions.

Coping skills are broken down into categories.

- Calming Skills – to calm you down.
- Distraction Skills – to redirect your attention.
- Releasing Skills – to express one's self through actions or communication.

Coping skills are used to build confidence, help

manage stress, help work through challenges, improves independence, help manage emotions, and improves behavior.

I have listed coping skills. Circle the ones that will work for you based on activities you enjoy doing. Fill in the blanks for any coping skills you plan on using that are not listed. Make realistic choices.

- Cry
- Scream
- Rest

- Deep Breathing
- Meditation
- Talk to someone
- Watch a movie
- Journaling
- Do a craft
- Group therapy
- Knit
- Cook
- Clean
- Do yoga
- Listen to music
- Read
- Praying
- Get a massage
- Exercise
- Be in nature
- Go to church
- Positive self-talk

- Take a break
- Sing
- Start a garden
- Play sports
- Slowly count to 10
- Write a letter
- Dance
- Think of someone you love
- Take pictures
- Drawing
- Hiking
- Hot bath
- Spa day
- Stretch
- Walk away
- Paint your nails
- Build with blocks
- Shopping
- Go on vacation

- Be assertive
- Spend time with family
- Use humor
- Painting a room
- Study the sky
- Spend time with pets
- Go to a gun range
- Aromatherapy
- Hug someone or pillow
- Go for a drive
- Read your bible
- Go for a bike ride
- Memorize a verse, poem, or song
- Look at old photos
- Rearrange furniture
- Make a healthy snack
- Sit in the sun
- Play pool
- Create a video

- Meet with friends for lunch or dinner
- Go to the library
- Research a topic of interest
- Make a gift for someone
- Play darts
- Blog
- Get enough sleep
- Socialize
- Face a fear
- Find a hobby
- Get in touch with your spirituality
- Acupuncture

Affirmations

Emotional support or encouragement

In this section, I would like for you to write daily affirmations for yourself that will help transition your negative thoughts into positive thoughts. That will help you feel motivated. That will help you feel good about yourself. That will help achieve your goal.

Affirmation should be not only read daily but the words must be spoken out loud. Hearing words out loud allows you to process what you are reading on another level. The more you see and hear it, the more you believe in it, the more it becomes reality. Once you have mastered your first set of affirmations, write new affirmations that will carry you to the next level of goals you want to achieve and of the things you want to overcome.

EX:

I am somebody.

I love myself.

I am beautiful.

I am a success.

I will not let anger get the best of me.

I am a survivor.

I will not let my past define my future.

I will forgive all who have hurt me.

I am a conqueror.

I am healed.

I have a purpose.

I will be a millionaire.

I will have my own business.

I am motivated.

I can do all things.

I will let nothing stand in my way.

I will never give up.

I matter.

I am great.

I am strong.

I will achieve my goals.

I will not let nothing stand in my way.

Write affirmations below:

| |
| |
| |
| |
| |

Change

Alter or modify

of

Environment

The surrounding or social and cultural conditions that influence the life of an individual or community

Environmental changes do not only include your physical surrounding. It also includes the company you keep. One of the biggest issues with the change of environment is that people don't know how to let go of poor relationships.   The friend you've had since childhood that does nothing but influence negativity in your life. The ex that you consider to be a friend when in reality they only want to feel like they hold some type of authority in your life. **THEY ARE NOT YOUR FRIEND.** The family members who smile in your face and talk about you soon as you leave. You don't have to be active in one another's life. It is perfectly fine to love family from a distance to protect your peace.

We all have places that we love to go to. But if those places are tied to negative emotions, it's time to learn to live without going to those places also. I often hear people say, "We have so many memories together", "We use to be here together all the time". But the key thing is that it is only memories that haven't faded out because you won't allow them to.

Instead of focusing on all the good times, you have shared with people, you have to remember why they are such a trigger for you. You must remember how much hurt they have caused you. You must remember how much drama they bring to your life.

Yes, you are to forgive them. But letting go of toxics never-ending situations is a major key to ultimate peace. Yes, we love people but that doesn't mean they are meant to be around forever. People come into your life in seasons to be a blessing. I only say blessing because the lesson that you learned in knowing them is a blessing.

The lesson could have made you wiser, stronger, more driven, etc. The question is how many times do you have to relive the lesson for it to become a blessing?

In this final section, I would like for you to write down every place and each person that needs to be removed from your environment. Do not hold back. For example, it could be your mother who is causing your life hell. Until she can respect the level of peace that you require, sorry momma but you must go as well.

Reflection

Serious thought or consideration

Please remember that life wasn't intended to be easy. The battles that we have faced in life are the tools we needed to be the best versions of ourselves. We are conquerors. We are survivors. We are strong. We are walking proof of change. We are walking proof that bad things don't last forever. We are wiser. We are of greatness. We are warriors. We are love. We are life. We are determined. We are driven. We are motivated.

We are achievers. We are chosen. We are believers. We are overcomers.

Life Coach Services

Do you want to know and understand your purpose?

Do you want to reach your full potential?

Do you desire success with no limits?

Do you want to gain control over your emotions?

Do you need a confidence boost?

Do you desire a clear

 understanding of the law of attraction?

Do you seek spiritual growth?

Do you just need peace of mind?

Are you trying to rebuild relationships?

Are you indecisive about making a decision?

Are you letting fear hold you back from living your dream life?

I AM HERE FOR YOU!!!

My core belief is "Life Is What You Make It". I am only a guide to help you reprogram your mind to overcome every obstacle within you that you feel is holding you back in life. The ultimate task is in your hands. The real question is, ARE YOU READY?

CONTACT ME NOW FOR YOUR FREE 10 MINUTE CONSULTAION

RHYTHMSOFLIFE.COACHING@GMAIL.COM

Made in the USA
Columbia, SC
23 October 2020